Steam Survivors

Steam Survivors

Roy Avis

Silver Link Publishing Ltd

First published in 2003

British Library Cataloguing in Publication Data

A catalogue record for this book is available from the British Library.

ISBN 1 85794 207 8

Silver Link Publishing Ltd
The Trundle
Ringstead Road
Great Addington
Kettering
Northants NN14 4BW

Tel/Fax: 01536 330588
email: sales@nostalgiacollection.com
Website: www.nostalgiacollection.com

Printed and bound in Great Britain

Page 1 **Shrewsbury:** One of Gresley's mighty 'A4s', No 60009 *Union of South Africa*, passes the county town of Salop with a Birmingham International to Liverpool Lime Street train. *2 March 2002*

Page 2 **Greenholme:** A big red 'un, one of Crewe's finest, back on the main line after being stored for many years at Bressingham museum: No 6233 *Duchess of Sutherland*, in LMS crimson lake livery, storms over Shap Fell with a Crewe to Carlisle train. *27 April 2002*

Below **Kettering Junction:** Taken with the old pre-war camera that whetted the author's appetite for steam photography is 'Jubilee' Class No 45618 *New Hebrides*, seen soon after nationalisation; rated 5XP by the old LMS and re-classified 6P by British Railways, the locomotive has a brand new number plate and the tender awaits re-lettering. Withdrawn at 17B (Burton) shed in February 1964, it was stored there until October, and was scrapped at Looms yard, Spondon, in November of that year. *Circa 1949*

Contents

Preface

The ever-changing face of railway technology is constantly with us, and some of the scenes depicted in this volume are already historic.

Obviously there is a need to bring equipment up to date, but where once a signal box and semaphore signalling added character to the background, there are now lineside weeds and overgrown embankments. Signal cabins are regarded with particular affection by steam enthusiasts; part of the pleasure is listening for the bell, which when answered will be followed by four more if it is an express passenger train, known in railway parlance as 'offering a train'. The bells raise expectancy in the photographer's mind as he watches the movement of the levers in the frame and contemplates which signals are being 'pulled off'. Some cabins occupy outposts in the bleakest places – Blea Moor, for example, on the Settle and Carlisle line.

Undoubtedly the 1990s were the most exciting years since the beginning of preserved main-line steam. Privatisation brought open access and the right to run almost anywhere on the national network, whatever the motive power. There were good reasons, of course, why steam had previously been restricted to well-chosen routes, with repeat itineraries avoiding the problems that occur with one-off charters. There are many in the upper hierarchies of railway administration who would be glad to see the back of main-line steam, and, given the problems they face, it is difficult to imagine why the tour operators and locomotive owners bother.

Anyone experiencing difficulties in obtaining details of steam railtours should consult the main-line diary in one of the various monthly magazines, where provisional dates and routes will be provided. Timings can be gained from the telephone hot-line of the Friends of the Main Line Steam Locomotive Operators; contact the Membership Secretary, FMSLO, 30 Whittington House, Hobs Road, Lichfield, Staffordshire WS13 6TB to join.

Great Western Railway locomotives

'City' Class

Above **Washwood Heath:** A familiar Birmingham landmark close to the M6 motorway, the giant gasometers dwarf No 3440 *City of Truro*, seen here with a Derby to Paddington train. As long ago as 1904 the locomotive achieved a claimed running speed of more than 100mph, but the record was never authenticated. *3 May 1992*

Above right **Fenny Compton:** Later the same day, on home territory, No 3440 heads south over former Great Western lines with the special for London Paddington. *3 May 1992*

Right **Aynho Junction:** Having replenished its water supplies at Banbury, *City of Truro* takes the up Bicester line with the Derby to Paddington train. This was the engine's last run before expiry of its main-line boiler certificate, but funds are being raised for renewal to MT276 standard in time to celebrate the centenary of the 100mph record.

MT 276 is the specification for overhaul and re-tubing of steam locomotives to main-line standards, with a boiler certificate valid for seven years. An extension of three years can be obtained, provided that a further re-tube and examination is carried out before the certificate expires. *3 May 1992*

'Hall' Class

Left **Penzance:** A northerly wind, a cold day, and a lot of smoke as Nos 4936 *Kinlet Hall* and 5029 *Nunney Castle* depart with the return working to Taunton of a special day excursion train. It was good to see that the pair were still in the correct formation, as they had been when they arrived at the resort nine days earlier, with the larger, more powerful of the two locomotives as the train engine. *16 April 2001*

Below **Bedwyn:** Usually a picturesque setting, the Kennet & Avon Canal is deserted, closed due to the outbreak of foot and mouth disease, as No 4936 passes with a Didcot to Taunton train. *17 March 2001*

Right **Henley-in-Arden:** On the North Warwickshire line, the signal box is Great Western but the semaphores are British Railways, probably London Midland Region, as No 4965 *Rood Ashton Hall* passes with a Stratford-upon-Avon to Birmingham Snow Hill train. *2 January 2000*

Below **Bearley Junction:** Almost 400 years after the death of the Bard, No 4965 is seen on the Stratford-upon-Avon branch, returning to Birmingham Snow Hill with 'The Shakespeare Express'. *4 June 2000*

Starcross: It is high tide in the Exe estuary, just beyond the Powderham Castle gatehouse, as No 4936 pilots No 5029, heading west with a Taunton to Penzance train. *7 April 2001*

Right **Penmaenmawr:** Somewhat bizarrely a 'Hall' was hired and renamed *Hogwarts Castle* for the 'Harry Potter' films. Still in red livery after playing its supporting role, No 5972 *Olton Hall* is seen just to the west of Penmaenbach Tunnel with a Carnforth to Holyhead special day excursion train. *28 April 2001*

Below **Greenholme:** In preservation Great Western locomotives have a poor record on routes north over the Cumbrian fells, although this pair gave a good account of themselves on the climb to Shap summit. Nos 4965 and 4936 approach Scotchman's Bridge in charge of a Crewe to Carlisle train. *18 May 2002*

'Castle' Class

Above **Kirkstall Junction:** No 5029 *Nunney Castle* passes on the down main line with a Leeds to Carlisle special. The engine was detached at Howe & Co's siding and the train proceeded diesel-hauled to Carlisle, there being insufficient clearance in the platforms at Carlisle station for the outside cylinders of the steam locomotive. *12 February 1994*

Below **Fairwood Junction:** No 5029 passes with a Paddington to Cranmore train. The Westbury avoiding line joins from the right. *8 October 1994*

Above **Paddington:** Emerging from beneath Brunel's fine arched station roof bays, No 5029 departs from Platform 10 on the down relief line with a Stratford-upon-Avon excursion train. *19 April 1992*

Right **Bearley Junction:** The signal box now controls the entire length of the busy Stratford-upon-Avon branch, although there was another cabin at the terminus when this photograph was taken. No 5029 heads the special day excursion train seen above leaving Paddington earlier in the day. *19 April 1992*

Above left **Worcester Shrub Hill:** No 5029 departs for Paddington with the return working of a special day excursion train. Just visible to the right of the smokebox door is the air-brake pump that was fitted to the locomotive during heavy maintenance for the renewal of its boiler certificate. *14 July 2001*

Left **Crofton:** Fitted in the traditional position, there being insufficient space available to hide it in the tender or elsewhere, the air-brake pump is in full view from this side as *Nunney Castle* passes with a Paddington to Paignton train; a badly clinkered fire was reported to be the cause of a late arrival at its destination. The line here closely follows the route of the Kennet & Avon Canal. *4 August 2001*

Above **Cogload Junction:** Constructed in 1931, the flyover carries the down Bristol to Exeter line over the Castle Cary and Langport route. No 5029 leans into the curve with a Westbury to Plymouth train. *17 February 1996*

'King Class'

Above **Saltash:** Suitably inscribed as a tribute to its great designer, the Royal Albert Bridge carries the only remaining main-line rail link into Cornwall. No 6024 *King Edward I* arrives on the Devonshire side with a Par to Didcot train. *30 May 1998*

Above right **Ferryside:** Running along a delightful stretch of the Carmarthenshire coast, but more than an hour late, No 6024 passes with a Newport (South Wales) to Fishguard Harbour train. *3 July 1999*

Right **Spooner Row:** No 6024 is heading a King's Cross to Norwich special train. Note the telegraph poles, now virtually extinct on the national railway network due to the proliferation of lineside ducting. *20 December 1998*

Above **Warwick:** Leaving the historic town in the distance, *King Edward I* climbs Hatton bank with a Paddington to Stratford-upon-Avon special day excursion train. *24 April 1994*

Below **Aynho Junction:** Slightly out of focus, but a sharp performance from No 6024 on a Stratford-upon-Avon to Didcot train, the return working of the special seen above on the outward trip. On this occasion steam gave way to diesel power at Didcot for the run to Paddington. *24 April 1994*

Right **Dorridge:** Having taken over the train that was brought in from Derby by a diesel, No 6024 crosses over to the up main as it departs for Didcot with a special day excursion.

The origin and destination of the trains featured in this volume are given for the steam-hauled sections only. Very few of the railtours are steam-hauled throughout – most have either diesel or electric traction included in the itinerary. *9 January 1993*

Below **Artengill:** Running late after an unscheduled stop at Kirkby Stephen due to low boiler pressure, *King Edward I* heads south with a Carlisle to Crewe train. *14 March 1998*

Above **Abergavenny:** Back on the main line after renewal of its MT276 certificate, No 6024 *King Edward I* gets under way again after being held at the signals with a Newport (South Wales) to Crewe train. The run incorporated a successful spark arrestor test on the locomotive. *21 February 1998*

Above right **Coldrenick:** There are more than 30 viaducts on the West of England main line in Cornwall, some of them like this one clearly visible from the A38 trunk road. No 6024 is westbound with an Exeter St David's to Penzance train. *19 September 1998*

Right **Newport (South Wales):** Arriving from Swansea with a Didcot train, No 6024 emerges into the daylight from Hillfield Tunnel; the special will be stopping at the station for the locomotive to replenish its water supplies. *22 May 1994*

'Modified Hall' Class

Above **Aynho Junction:** Built by British Railways at Swindon to Great Western Railway design, No 6998 *Burton Agnes Hall* makes a rare main-line appearance, in charge of a Didcot to Stratford-upon-Avon special train. *14 March 1993*

Above right **Hatton:** Later the same day, having stopped at Banbury to take water, No 6998 makes good progress up the bank with the Didcot to Stratford-upon-Avon special day excursion train. *14 March 1993*

Right **Bearley:** Just before sunset at the former Bearley East Junction site, No 6998 is returning to Didcot from Stratford-upon-Avon with the same train. *14 March 1993*

'Manor Class'

Left **Droitwich Spa:** Just over 16 miles from its destination, No 7802 *Bradley Manor* is on the final leg of a loaded test run from Stourbridge Junction to Newport (South Wales) and return. *19 May 1995*

Below **Caersws:** After a brief stop, No 7819 *Hinton Manor* departs with a Shrewsbury to Barmouth train. The line is controlled by the radio electronic token block system, but semaphore signals remain in use at the manned level crossing. *16 June 1991*

Above **Cogload Junction:** 'Grade segregated' the road builders would probably call it, but the Great Western made abundant use of flyovers long before the first motorway was constructed. No 7802 takes the flyover with a Bristol Temple Meads to Plymouth train. *22 January 2000*

Below **Dawlish:** Later in the day, No 7802 bursts out of the short Clerk's Tunnel at Horse Cove with the Bristol Temple Meads to Plymouth special; the milepost is 207 miles from Paddington, via Box. *22 January 2000*

Southern Railway
locomotives

'S15' Class

Above **Waterloo:** Built by the Southern Railway at Eastleigh to a modified London & South Western Railway design, No 828 departs for Salisbury with a special day excursion train. *15 May 1994*

Above right **Aynho Junction:** By this time the signal cabin was out of use and abandoned, control of the junction being from Banbury South. No 828 passes with a Didcot to Derby train. *23 March 1994*

Right **Warnham:** Stopping to replenish its water supplies, No 828 arrives from Portsmouth Harbour with a London day excursion train. At least 3,000 gallons will be needed to fill the tender – standard gauge steam locomotives running on the main line consume about 50 gallons per mile. *11 February 1996*

'West Country' Class

Left **Little Salkeld:** Introduced by the Southern Railway and rebuilt by British Railways, No 34027 *Taw Valley* passes with a Carlisle to Bradford Forster Square train. Confused with Langwathby and shown as still open on the 1988 Ordnance Survey Landranger Sheet No 90, the station is actually closed – a rare mistake by a respected organisation. *5 March 1994*

Below **Exeter Central:** After stopping to detach a diesel banker from the rear, No 34027 erupts into action as it departs with an Exeter St David's to Salisbury train. Desecrated by the graffiti artists, the signal cabin is out of use. *19 September 1993*

Above **Guildford North Junction:** On the Portsmouth Direct Line, which was electrified long before the Bulleid 'light Pacifics' were introduced, No 34027 approaches with a London Victoria to Fratton train. *2 February 1997*

Below **Barry Docks:** No. 34027 passes the former Port Authority building with a Bristol Temple Meads to Swansea train. The high-level sidings have all been removed, but the single low-level line to the No 2 Dock remains in use. *6 April 1996*

Left **Offord D'Arcy:** Running beside the River Great Ouse with the 'Lincolnshire Belle' steam special, No 34027 *Taw Valley* never got beyond Cambridgeshire due to a hot axlebox on the tender. The train, however, completed its journey diesel-hauled. *18 July 1998*

Below **North Queensferry:** Opened in 1890, the Forth Bridge is one of Britain's most notable railway engineering structures. *Taw Valley* crosses with an Edinburgh-Perth private charter train to launch the authoress J. K. Rowling's then latest 'Harry Potter' book. *11 July 2000*

Right **Wateringbury:** At Wilson's occupation crossing No 34016 *Bodmin*, displaying the appropriate Southern Railway headlamp disc code, heads a Maidstone West to Tonbridge train; the milepost measures 39 miles from Charing Cross, via Chelsfield. *27 August 2000*

Below **Bransty:** No 34027 is seen at Redness Point, not very far from Whitehaven on the Cumbrian Coast line, with a Workington to Crewe train. *14 October 2000*

'Merchant Navy' Class

Above **London Victoria:** 'Dinner in the diner, nothing could be finer' – No 35028 *Clan Line* approaches Ebury Bridge with a VSOE Surrey Hills special luncheon train from Guildford. The former Battersea power station building is in the background. *4 April 1997*

Above right **Guildford New Line Junction:** The first preserved main-line steam locomotive to be fitted with an air-brake pump, No 35028 threads its way across the junction with a VSOE special luncheon train of air-braked Pullman coaches.

Most steam locomotives are vacuum-braked only, but with very little dual-braked coaching stock remaining on the national railway network, the majority of main-line steam engines are now air-braked. There is nothing new about air-braking for steam locomotives of course, elderly Isle of Wight residents for instance will remember the familiar beat of the Westinghouse pumps on the island's Adams tank engines, although the modern variety are less noisy. *23 May 1997*

Right **Betchworth:** No 35028 is seen at the head of another special luncheon train. The station has been refurbished to a very high standard, a credit to those responsible – hopefully the vandals will stay away. *6 January 1997*

Left **Southampton:** Displaying the Southern Region headlamp disc code for a special boat express, No 35028 arrives from London Victoria with a train for the QEII terminal. The lavish former South Western Hotel building is in the background. *4 January 1996*

Below **Worting Junction:** Joining the Bournemouth main line at Battledown flyover, *Clan Line* is on its way up from Salisbury with 'The Woking Centenarian'. *24 March 1995*

Right **Canterbury West:** Engulfed in steam from the open cylinder drain cocks only a split second earlier, re-built Bulleid No 35005 *Canadian Pacific* leaves with the empty coaching stock of a special day excursion. The train returned to London via Dover later in the day. *19 February 2000*

Below **Aynho Junction:** No 35005 passes with a Birmingham to Bristol train. The Southern Region headlamp disc codes are not of any significance here, and never have been – perhaps they forgot to remove them after the trip to the Kent coast three weeks earlier. *11 March 2000*

Above **Salisbury:** No 35028 *Clan Line* departs with a London Victoria to Westbury train. The magnificent cathedral spire is England's tallest. *25 March 2000*

Above right **Rugeley Town:** In the shadow of the power station, *Canadian Pacific* crosses five arches bridge, on the Cannock and Rugeley line, with a Birmingham International to Chester train. *16 December 2000*

Right **Guildford North Junction:** Displaying the Southern Region headlamp disc code of a Salisbury and Portsmouth Harbour train, No 35028 passes on the down Cobham line with 'The Solent and Sarum' railtour. *21 November 1998*

Left **Kensington Olympia:** No 35028 arrives with a London Victoria to Bath special day excursion train. A whiff of steam from the air-brake pump, located in the tender, can be seen above the first coach. *5 November 1997*

Below **Canterbury West:** On an empty coaching stock movement, No 35028 displays the Southern Region headlamp disc code for a London Victoria to Dover train. *24 January 1998*

Above **Irchester:** Coasting down the grade from Sharnbrook summit towards Wellingborough on its way north, No 35005 approaches the start of a temporary speed restriction with an Alton to Leicester special day excursion train. *29 September 2001*

Below **Waterloo:** Displaying a 'Bournemouth Belle' headboard, No 35028 departs with a Southampton train – on the Windsor Reversible line! *4 February 2001*

London Midland & Scottish Railway locomotives

2MT Class

Above **Heighington:** Where it all began – George Stephenson's engine *Locomotion* was placed on the tracks here in 1825, ready for the official opening of the Stockton & Darlington Railway. Almost 170 years later, No 46441 departs with a Darlington Bank Top to Stanhope special train. *31 December 1994*

Above right **Miles Platting:** Built by British Rail at Crewe to an LMS design, No 46441 passes the signal box with a Bolton to Sheffield train, commemorating the centenary of the Hope Valley line. *26 June 1994*

Right **Frosterley:** The now closed Wear Valley line, where passenger traffic ceased as long ago as 1953, is retained out of use, but the tracks to Eastgate cement works remain. No 46441 is seen again with the Darlington to Stanhope special. *31 December 1994*

5MT Class 'Mogul'

Left **Conwy:** Beneath the drum towers and battlements of the castle, 'Mogul' No 2968 passes with a Crewe to Holyhead train. *19 October 1997*

Below **Lydgate:** No 2968 heads a Crewe, Blackburn and York railtour, running very slowly down the grade due to a permanent way restriction. *8 March 1997*

Above **Cynghordy:** Overloaded and making very slow progress, No 2968 slogs up the grade with a Port Talbot to Shrewsbury special just before grinding to a halt when the brakes came on due to low steam pressure – 'fail safe' they call it. *18 October 1997*

Right **Sugar Loaf:** After twice being brought to a stand on the climb with the Port Talbot to Shrewsbury special seen above at Cynghordy viaduct, No 2968 is about to enter the 1,001-yard tunnel leading to the summit. It would not normally be possible to get both these shots of the same train. *18 October 1997*

5MT Class 'Black Five'

Tebay: In the Lune Gorge, masquerading as No 45157, its reporting number chalked on the smokebox door, No 45407 heads south with a Glasgow to Crewe train. One of only four named 'Black Fives', No 45157 *The Glasgow Highlander* was withdrawn at 65B Saint Rollox shed in December 1962, where it was stored until June 1963, finally being scrapped at the Arnott Young yard, Troon, the following month. *29 May 2000*

Above **St Pancras:** Passing the renowned gasometers, No 44767 departs for Crewe. This was believed to have been the first steam-hauled train to leave the terminus for 26 years. *22 April 1995*

Below **Irchester:** Heading south towards the Bedfordshire border and Sharnbrook summit, No 44767 crosses the River Nene with a Stockport to London St Pancras train. Only one goods line remains open on the elevated formation, following de-quadrupling. *25 March 1995*

Left **Holywell Junction:** Running in LMS livery, No 5407 (BR number 45407) passes the closed station with 'The North Wales Coast Express', a Crewe to Holyhead train. Partly paid for by the North Wales coast resorts, which helped to finance a new triangle at Valley for the turning of engines, British Rail entered into a three-year agreement to run this train three times a week during the summer season. Valley is probably better known for the air-sea rescue services provided by its local base. *27 August 1989*

Below **Knucklas:** No 44767 struggles up the grade with a Shrewsbury to Carmarthen train. The viaduct is the architectural masterpiece of the Central Wales line. *23 May 1993*

Right **Shrewsbury:** Running as No 45157 *The Glasgow Highlander* after a trip to Scotland four weeks earlier, No 45407 passes Sutton Bridge Junction on its way to Newport (South Wales) with 'The Welsh Dragon' special. *24 June 2000*

Below **Rugeley Town:** At the limit of electrification from the Trent Valley main line, No 45110 crosses five arches bridge on the Cannock and Rugeley line with a Birmingham to Chester train. *18 December 1999*

Bristol Temple Meads: Nos 45407 and 45110 depart for Plymouth, double-heading a special day excursion train. Built jointly by the Great Western Railway in partnership with the Bristol & Exeter Railway and the Midland Railway, the station is on the former connecting curve from the GWR to the B&E line. *15 August 1999*

Right **Culgaith:** 'Shovel all the coal in, gotta keep it rollin'…' – fuel consumption can vary according to route, load and footplate crew, but normally 30-plus miles to the ton would be expected. No 44871 pilots No 45596 on a Carlisle to Leeds train, commemorating the 25th anniversary of the '15 Guinea Special' end-of-steam specials of 1968 – unfortunately it was necessary to increase the fares. *11 August 1993*

Below **Miles Platting:** No 44767 takes the Manchester and Normanton line with empty coaching stock for Castleton sidings; the Ashton-under-Lyne branch is in the foreground. *18 March 1995*

Above **Peak Forest:** Apart from the removal of the lime kilns, and the addition of floodlighting in the yard, little has changed here since 1947, when the LMS published a book entitled *The Track of the Peak Expresses*, covering the route from Manchester Central to London St Pancras. Within another 2½ miles, however, the tracks to the south have been lifted, and the train can only proceed over the former branch line to Buxton, where water will be taken. No 45110 is on a Derby to Crewe railtour. *5 February 2000*

Left **Buxton:** The station is a terminus, but there is a direct connection from the former LNWR Buxton branch to the High Peak Junction line, and there is also access, through the up exchange sidings, to the branch from Peak Forest on the former Midland main line. No 45110 departs with the railtour seen above at Peak Forest earlier in the day. *5 February 2000*

Above **Wrawby Junction:** No 44767 heads a Crewe to Cleethorpes train past a plethora of semaphores, and one of the largest remaining signal cabins on the former Great Central system. *20 May 1995*

Below **Barnetby:** Passing the derelict maltings, No 45407 leaves with a Castleton to Cleethorpes train. The semaphore signals are only a part of the vast display here and at nearby Wrawby Junction. *27 March 1999*

Greenholme: There's a westerly wind and a welcome break in the clouds over the Cumbrian fells as No 45407 (45157) heads north with a Preston to Edinburgh train, assisted at the rear by No 76079, the first Shap banker for more than 30 years. *6 October 2001*

Right **Poulton-le-Fylde:** The locomotive crew of No 45110, on a Shrewsbury to Blackpool North train, have discarded their orange jackets, and there is very little, if anything, to indicate that we no longer live in a steam world. *17 October 1998*

Below **Glenfinnan:** No 44767 arrives with a Fort William to Mallaig train, the sound of the engine reverberating around the hills as it climbs the last half-mile to the station. *3 July 1997*

Left **Ashton Moss North Junction:** The diesel driver waves to his colleagues on the footplate of No 45407 (as No 45157), with a trans-Pennine railtour. *20 January 2001*

Below **Clayton:** Note the somewhat unusual place to build a house, above the tunnel between the towers of the castellated north portal, as No 45407 (45157), the first main-line steam engine to be fitted with Train Protection and Warning System (TPWS), bursts out into the daylight in charge of a Brighton to London Victoria train. A date has been set by which TPWS will become obligatory, and there will be no exemption for steam. *9 February 2002*

Above **Brundall:** There are plenty of day excursion trains over this route, but not very many of them are steam-hauled. Running once more as No 45157, No 45407 passes with a Great Yarmouth to Liverpool Street special. *5 May 2001*

Below **Manningtree:** Later the same day, approaching one of East Anglia's most important junctions, No 45407 crosses the River Stour estuary with the Great Yarmouth to Liverpool Street special. *5 May 2001*

Hartford Junction: Still running as No 45157, almost three months after its change of identity, No 45407 heads north on the former LNWR main line with a train from Crewe to Carnforth, Skipton, and the Grassington branch. *19 August 2000*

Above **Blackpool North:** Formerly known as Talbot Road, the carriage sidings here remain in situ, but the engine shed site, behind the signal box, is now a residential development. No 45407 (as 45157) departs for Carlisle with a special day excursion train. *22 July 2000*

Below **Settle Junction:** The layout here is designed to give northbound trains a flying start on the 15-mile climb to Blea Moor summit over the Settle and Carlisle route. No 45407 weaves its way across the junction from the Morecambe line with the special for Skipton and the Grassington branch seen opposite at Hartford Junction earlier in the day. *19 August 2000*

6P 'Jubilee' Class

Conwy: One of the very few engines in its class to be fitted with a double chimney, plainly visible in this side view, No 45596 *Bahamas* passes the 13th-century castle with a Crewe to Holyhead train. *27 May 1991*

Right **Bangor:** A modest enough timepiece as clocks go, but infinitely superior to the digital instruments now commonplace throughout the network – it's 13.48 and *Bahamas* is running 33 minutes late with a Crewe to Holyhead train. *19 August 1992*

Below **Holyhead:** No 45596 storms away from the terminus with a Holyhead to Crewe train. The former engine shed site, now a locomotive inspection point, is on the right. *10 October 1993*

Artengill: No 45596 heads north with a Keighley to Carlisle train at a splendid setting in the Yorkshire Dales. *4 October 1992*

Right **Skipton:** *Bahamas* departs for Barrow-in-Furness with a special day excursion train. There are regular passenger services to Leeds, Bradford, Lancaster, Morecambe and Carlisle from this busy station. *1 August 1993*

Below **Seamer West:** No 45596 passes with a Bradford Forster Square to Scarborough train. This was the engine's last railtour before its seven-year main-line boiler certificate expired. *18 September 1994*

8P 'Princess Royal' Class

Above **Garsdale:** No 46203 *Princess Margaret Rose* crosses Dandry Mire Viaduct with a Blackburn to Carlisle train. The station here was originally called Hawes Junction, being the point at which the former Hawes branch left the main line, and there is still a small place of worship named Hawes Junction chapel, quite close to the railway bridge over the A684 road. *13 August 1994*

Below **Smardale:** There are two viaducts here, the other being on the dismantled Eden Valley line. No 46203 coasts down the grade on the Settle and Carlisle route with a Blackburn to Appleby train. *1 June 1991*

Right **Rhyl:** No 46203 *Princess Margaret Rose* passes with a Holyhead to Crewe train. A fine array of semaphore signals remain on the gantry, although some have been removed due to rationalisation of the track layout. *18 June 1995*

Below **Shrewsbury:** With very few turntables remaining on the network, destinations having track layouts where engines can be turned are a popular choice for steam specials. Having arrived from Crewe chimney-first, No 6201 *Princess Elizabeth* reverses along Abbey Foregate curve on its way round the triangle of lines surrounding Severn Bridge signal box; when it runs forward again, towards the station, it will be facing in the opposite direction to which it arrived. *6 May 1992*

Above **Ais Gill:** During a bright period between flurries of snow, No 46203 battles its way towards the summit with a Carlisle to Sheffield train. *19 March 1994*

Below **Prestatyn:** The locomotive's diamond jubilee special earlier in the year was cancelled due to a high lineside fire risk. Displaying the headboard provided for the occasion, but never used, No 46203 passes with a Crewe to Holyhead train. *28 October 1995*

Steam survivors in colour

Beattock: Believed to be the first time since 1962 that a 'Princess Royal' Class locomotive had tackled the climb, No 6201 *Princess Elizabeth* is seen at Harthope with a Carlisle to Perth train. Later the same day, after a delay in turning and servicing the locomotive, the train went on to Edinburgh Waverley, arriving there in the early hours of Sunday morning. Take a look at page 33 of *The Glory of Steam* by Stephen Crook (SLP 1 85794 178 0). *28 September 2002*

Ais Gill: At the classic location for photographing southbound trains on the Settle and Carlisle line, No 6233 *Duchess of Sutherland* crosses the famous narrow mountain stream with a Carlisle to Derby special. At one time under threat of closure, there has been a resurgence in freight traffic over the route in recent years. *20 July 2002*

Longport Junction: On the Macclesfield and Colwich line, a few miles to the north of Stoke-on-Trent, a city that had a 'Coronation' Class 'Pacific' named after it, No 6233 *Duchess of Sutherland* passes with a Derby to Blackpool special day excursion train. *13 April 2002*

Harringworth Viaduct: This is the longest all-masonry viaduct on the national railway network, built by the Midland Railway to carry the Kettering and Manton line across the Welland valley. Kept open by traffic from the north to the nearby Corby steelworks, trains of any sort are a rarity, let alone an ex-LNER 'A4' 'Pacific'-hauled charter. No 60009 passes over with a Kettering to York special. *10 May 2003*

Shrewsbury: Former LNER 'A4' No 60009 *Union of South Africa* rounds the Abbey Foregate curve with a Hereford to Bescot special train. The floodlights at Gay Meadow football ground, where Everton were defeated a week later, can be seen to the left. *28 December 2002*

Corrour: North British-built locomotives 'K1' No 62005 (as 62012) and 'B1' 61264 (as 61243) make their way up to the summit with a Fort William to Bridge of Orchy private charter train. One of Britain's most remote railway locations, the station here is more than 7 miles from the nearest road. *6 October 2002*

Upper Tyndrum: Both locomotives working hard, the same pair head a Fort William to Crianlarich private charter train at County March summit. Allocated to Fort William during the early 1960s, the real No 62012 was withdrawn at Sunderland in May 1967, and scrapped at Draper's yard, Hull, on 28 August of that year. Withdrawn at Ayr in May 1964, No 61243 was scrapped at the Arnott Young, West of Scotland shipbreakers' yard, Troon. *5 October 2002*

Tebay: Back on the national rail network following renewal of its boiler certificate, No 6201 *Princess Elizabeth* heads south through the Lune Gorge with a Carlisle to Preston train, the locomotive's first main-line railtour for approximately nine years. *11 May 2002*

Right **Blea Moor:** Beyond the summit, located inside the tunnel, No 46203 emerges into the daylight with a Nottingham to Carlisle train. The weather is bitterly cold, and a trace of snow remains on the fells. *9 March 1996*

Below **Mostyn:** Viewed from the quayside, *Princess Margaret Rose* passes with a Crewe to Holyhead train. The docks are closed for the weekend and the signal box is switched out. *6 September 1992*

8P 'Coronation' Class

Above **Scarborough:** No 46229 *Duchess of Hamilton* departs for Sheffield with the return working of a special day excursion train. There will be no design award for the engineer who decided to erect the lighting column next to the signal gantry – listed Grade II, the gantry can be removed but not destroyed. *7 October 1995*

Below **Seamer West:** No 46229 is seen again approaching Scarborough with a train from Preston. The semaphore signals and signal box have now been removed, victims of Railtrack's EROS programme – Economy through Rationalisation of Signalling. *30 March 1996*

Right **Gaerwen Junction:** Just before 10 o'clock in the morning, with the Queen and Duke of Edinburgh on board, No 6233 *Duchess of Sutherland* passes with the Royal Train on its way from Holyhead to Llanfairpwll, for an official visit to Beaumaris Castle as part of the Golden Jubilee tour. This was the first ever steam-hauled Royal Train in the preservation era. *11 June 2002*

Below **Ais Gill:** No 46229 pounds its way towards the summit with a Carlisle to Blackburn train. Wild Boar Fell, as ever, is in the background. *5 June 1993*

Left **Huddersfield:** About to plunge into the longer Huddersfield North Tunnel, No 6233 emerges from the short Gledholt North Tunnel at Springwood Junction with a Liverpool Lime Street to York train. Joining from the left is the Penistone branch, and there are still two tracks through Huddersfield South tunnel following de-quadrupling; all of the tunnels here were originally double-track. *9 March 2002*

Below **Toton Yard:** On a loaded test run that ended in failure due to a leakage in the air-brake system, *Duchess of Sutherland* passes with a Derby to Sheffield train. Ratcliffe power station is just visible through the clouds. *18 July 2001*

Right **Pontrilas:** Viewed from the garden of the former station house, where waiting photographers were provided with free tea and biscuits by the friendly couple living there, No 46229 *Duchess of Hamilton* approaches with a Shrewsbury to Reading train. *2 November 1996*

Below **Euston:** Looking down Camden bank through the mass of gantries and wires that provide the power for the modern railway, No 6233 blasts its way past the carriage sheds with a London to Derby train. *15 December 2001*

8F Class

Above **Castleford:** At the small Yorkshire town famous for its 'Tigers' Rugby League team, passengers waiting for a local train observe the sedate progress of No 48151 with a Carnforth to Scarborough special. There is hardly a whiff of smoke from the chimney. *25 September 1993*

Above right **Mouldsworth Junction:** Sister locomotive No 48773 passes with a Shrewsbury to Blackburn train. Renovation of the signal box has been detrimental to its appearance. *1 February 1992*

Right **Long Preston:** Making steady progress during a period of high lineside fire risk, No 48151 passes with a Hellifield to Carlisle train. Thankfully the sparks were all burned out well before they reached the ground. *12 July 1996*

Lydgate: In typical Yorkshire surroundings, on the way up to Copy Pit summit, Nos 48773 and 45407 double-head a York to Crewe train out of Kitson Wood Tunnel and across the viaduct. *17 April 1999*

Right **Eskmeals:** No 48151 heads the return working, from Sellafield to Carnforth, of a special that should have gone to Carlisle, but the venue was changed at short notice due to operational difficulties. *31 May 1997*

Below **Lickey Incline:** Having regained its composure after a slip, No 48773 slogs past, unassisted, with a Gloucester to Tyseley train. *2 January 1999*

Glenfinnan: Built on a curve overlooking Loch Shiel, the viaduct is one of the earliest examples of concrete construction. No 48151 crosses with a Fort William to Mallaig train. *25 September 1998*

Above **Auch:** More than a mile from the A82 trunk road, this is a location unlikely to be listed in the gazetteer of your road atlas. No 48151, running tender-first, crosses Horseshoe Viaduct with a Fort William to Oban train. *25 September 1999*

Below **Oban:** No 48151 propels the empty coaching stock of a Taynuilt train into the station. The building on the hilltop overlooking the town is McCaig's Tower, a well-known Scottish landmark. *26 September 1999*

Left **Scarborough:** Exactly what the Environmental Health Officer's report would have said, had he been required to submit one, we will never know – No 48151 pollutes the North Yorkshire skies departing for Carnforth with a special day excursion train. *6 May 2000*

Below **Ashton Moss North Junction:** No 48773 takes the curve on to the Oldham, Ashton and Guide Bridge line, circumnavigating Greater Manchester, with a Crewe, Buxton and Derby railtour. *1 April 2000*

Above **Eskmeals:** Observed from the coast road at a time when access to the countryside was restricted due to the foot and mouth disease crisis, No 48151 crosses the estuary with a Sellafield to Carnforth train. *7 May 2001*

Right **Garsdale:** Logistic solutions No 48151 heads north with a Ribblehead Quarry to Carlisle Kingmoor loaded ballast train, the summit at Ais Gill just over 2 miles away. *19 December 2000*

London & North Eastern Railway locomotives

'A2' Class

Above **Blackpool North:** Well short of the output of the famous Gresley-Beyer Peacock 'Garratt', but with a claimed tractive effort of 40,430lb, the most powerful British steam passenger locomotive ever built, No 60532 *Blue Peter*, departs for Nuneaton with the return working of a special day excursion train. *26 May 2001*

Left **Seamer West:** Built by British Railways at Doncaster to an LNER design, and carrying a 50A York shed plate on its smokebox door, No 60532 leaves Scarborough with a York train. *2 May 1993*

Right **Blea Moor:** On a day so hot that the signalman is sunbathing, No 60532 passes with a Blackburn to Carlisle train. The signal cabin is in a very remote area, not connected to the main services, and water supplies for tea-making, etc, are delivered by rail. *13 June 1992*

Below **Garsdale:** With a few thousand more gallons in its tender than when it arrived, *Blue Peter* departs with a Carlisle to Blackburn train. Unpaid volunteers have maintained the water supply here since the end of the steam era. *15 August 1992*

'A3' Class

Above **Paddington:** Regarded as a 'foreign' locomotive by the old railwaymen on the Great Western in the days of the 'Big Four' grouping companies, there are no such prejudices in these politically correct times, however, as No 4472 *Flying Scotsman* departs for Stratford-upon-Avon with a special day excursion train. *16 February 1992*

Left **Fenny Compton:** A common occurrence today, but back in 1934, when *Flying Scotsman* became the first steam locomotive to officially reach 100mph, it was an impressive enough running speed. Giving a performance to match its reputation, No 4472 heads the Stratford-upon-Avon special day excursion train seen above leaving Paddington earlier in the day. *16 February 1992*

Above **Ely Dock Junction:** No 4472 passes with a Kings Lynn to Cambridge train, the first steam special of a series run that day to commemorate electrification of the line. *19 October 1991*

Below **Llandudno:** Framed by the signal gantry, *Flying Scotsman* leaves the terminus in back gear with a late summer bank holiday special from Crewe. There are no turning facilities available here for the engine, so the train is being towed out by a diesel at the other end – note the red tail lamp. *26 August 1991*

Left **London Victoria:** On the up Chatham slow line, No 4472 approaches Ebury Bridge with a train from Yeovil Junction. The former Battersea power station chimneys have long been redundant, but there is a whiff of smoke from the engine as it passes the carriage sheds. *27 November 1999*

Below **Aynho Junction:** Running 1 hour 40 minutes late due to a delay in the completion of overnight civil engineering works, No 4472 passes with a London Euston to Stratford-upon-Avon train. *19 December 1999*

Right **Rugby:** Once a very busy station, with branch lines to Leicester, Market Harborough and Leamington Spa, now the bay platforms are empty and the only action is on the down main as No 4472 passes with a Milton Keynes to Shrewsbury train. *7 October 1999*

Below **Offord D'Arcy:** This was a familiar route for *Flying Scotsman* in its heyday, but it is seen here suffering the indignity of running on the slow line with a York to King's Cross train. *11 July 1999*

Left **Kingussie:** This delightful little station, with a passing loop, is on a single-line section of the route. After waiting for an up freight to proceed in the opposite direction, *Flying Scotsman* departs for Inverness in charge of a private charter train. *19 October 2000*

Below **Druimachdair:** At the highest point on the national railway network, 1,484 feet above sea level in the Scottish highlands, No 4472 storms over the top with an Inverness to Edinburgh private charter train. *20 October 2000*

Right **Chester-le-Street:** On the route of the 'Flying Scotsman' express train, which still operates every day between King's Cross and Edinburgh, the steam locomotive of the same name, No 4472., passes with an Edinburgh to York private charter train. *21 October 2000*

Below **Offord D'Arcy:** Known locally as Gills footpath crossing, it is controlled by miniature red/green lights. Four tracks are a lot to cross on a high-speed line, and the King's Cross to Lincoln special day excursion behind No 4472 was already in sight, just beyond the church, when the warning light came on. *10 December 2000*

Left **Worting Junction:** Famous locomotive, famous flyover – No 4472 leaves the Bournemouth main line for the Basingstoke and Exeter route at Battledown, on its way from London Victoria to Salisbury with a special day excursion train. *25 May 2002*

Below **Malton:** The box junction at the level crossing would appear to be completely ineffective, or maybe the car driver was hoping to get a better view of No 4472 as it passes with a Scarborough to King's Cross special. *17 June 2001*

Right **Mitre Bridge:** On the West London line, No 4472 crosses the Great Western main line with a London Victoria to Westbury train, a scene reminiscent of the Great Central's 'birdcage bridge' at Rugby in LNER days. *4 April 2001*

Below **Newark:** Probably most, if not all, of the 'A3s' crossed the old bridge here, but now, following regeneration by Railtrack, only the *Scotsman* remains to test the new multi-million-pound structure across the River Trent, heading the Scarborough to King's Cross special seen opposite at Malton. *17 June 2001*

'A4' Class

Above **Stirling:** No 60009 *Union of South Africa* is on former Caledonian lines with a Cumbernauld to Perth train, one of a series for crew training, postponed earlier in the year due to problems with the engine. *16 October 1993*

Below **Stirling:** No 60009 departs with a Perth to Cumbernauld train, the last in the series of ScotRail locomotive crew training specials. *30 October 1993*

Above **Sheriff Brow:** Another splendid setting in the Yorkshire Dales, as former LNER locomotive No 4498 (British Railways No 60007) *Sir Nigel Gresley* tackles the 'Long Drag' with a Blackburn to Carlisle train. *9 April 1994*

Below **Greenholme:** Within a few hundred yards of the Westmorland motorway service area, where there is a good view of the line from the restaurant, No 60007 storms towards Shap summit with a Preston to Carlisle train. *8 March 1997*

Left **Hull Paragon:** Slipping and belching smoke, No 60007 makes a dramatic departure for King's Cross with a special day excursion train. *28 September 1997*

Below **King's Cross:** After a stoppage of 20 minutes between the tunnels at Belle Isle due to the brakes dragging, *Sir Nigel Gresley* gets under way again on the down slow line with a London to Scarborough train. *6 June 1999*

Right **King's Cross:** *Sir Nigel Gresley* emerges from Gasworks Tunnel and makes an early arrival with a train from Newcastle after a trouble-free run along the former LNER main line. *11 June 1995*

Below **Newcastle-upon-Tyne:** Viewed from the castle keep, No 60007 departs with a train for Edinburgh on the down north line; the lines to Gateshead and Sunderland leave to the left. *29 April 1995*

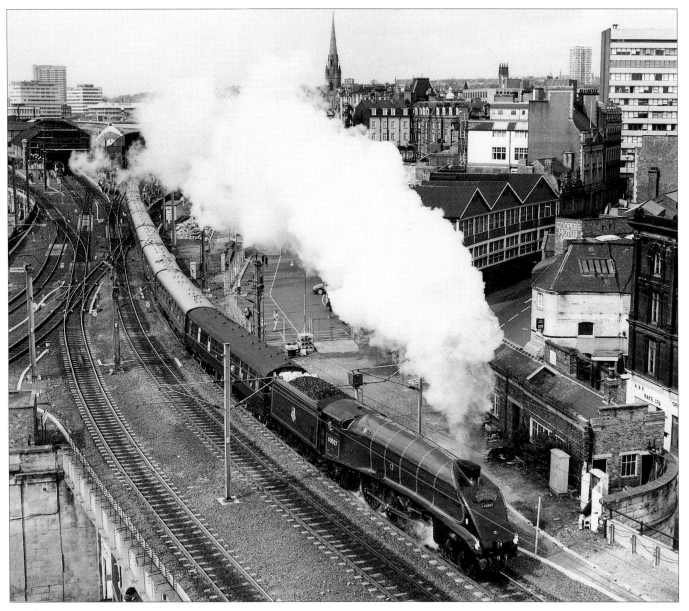

Left **Moreton-in-Marsh:** Stopping to collect the token for the single-line section to Evesham, No 60009 *Union of South Africa* arrives with a Paddington to Worcester Shrub Hill train, a London & North Eastern interloper on the Cotswold line. *22 June 2002*

Below **Hexham:** At the head of a York to Carlisle train, No 60007 passes one of the two remaining elevated former North Eastern Railway signal cabins on the Newcastle and Carlisle line – the other is at Wylam. *25 October 1997*

Above **Chirk:** 'Croeso i Cymru' – No 60009 crosses the Welsh border with a Hereford to Chester train. And 'Welcome to England' narrow-boat, travelling in the opposite direction on the Shropshire Union Canal. *25 April 1992*

Below **Beattock:** No 60007 tackles the legendary northbound climb with a Carlisle to Edinburgh train. Construction of the A74(M) motorway extension progresses on the hillside. *31 October 1998*

'B1' Class

Left **Scout Green:** Back-to-back performances from Nos 61264 and 62005, on their way to Scotland with a Carnforth to Mossend Yard empty coaching stock movement. *13 June 2001*

Below **Manningtree:** No 61264 rumbles across the Stour estuary bridge with a Liverpool Street to Lowestoft train. Diesel power took over at Norwich, due to an overheated driving wheel bearing on the steam locomotive. *10 November 2001*

Right **Oakham:** No 61264 visits the county town of Rutland – now re-instated as England's smallest shire – with an Ely to Derby train. The signal box is one of the best remaining examples of former Midland Railway cabins on Network Rail lines. *19 May 2001*

Below **Mallaig:** On a day when all services were steam-operated to commemorate the centenary of the line, No 61264 departs with a ScotRail train for Fort William, the first ever so-called 'Plandampf' on the national railway network, ie steam operation of normal passenger services. *2 October 2001*

'K1' Class

Darlington: Running as No 2005, in LNER livery, No 62005 departs for Eastgate 25 minutes late with the 14.30 special. *28 March 1993*

Right **Harrow-on-the-Hill:** On the tenth anniversary of 'Steam on the Met', No 62005 leaves for Watford on the local line. Most of the smoke is from the engine of a simultaneous departure on the northbound main line. *30 May 1999*

Below **Fort William:** Introduced by British Railways, as a Peppercorn development of Thompson's two-cylinder design, a total of 70 'K1' Class locomotives were built. No 62005 departs for Mallaig with a private charter train. *1 October 2001*

'V2' Class

Left **Miles Platting:** As No 4771 *Green Arrow* reaches the top of the bank from Manchester Victoria with a Carnforth to Crewe train the safety valves lift unexpectedly. Numbered 60800 by British Railways, the engine is the only preserved example of its class. *5 August 1991*

Below **Greenholme:** Back on the main line following renewal of its boiler certificate, No 60800 storms past with a train from Preston, which returned south over the Settle and Carlisle route. *3 October 1998*

Above **Fenny Compton:** Bedecked in bunting, No 60800 passes with a Sheffield to Marylebone train. There is still a trace of snow on the buffers from wintry showers further north. *6 March 1999*

Below **Langham Junction:** A rare glimpse of steam on the Syston and Peterborough line – No 60800 heads a special day excursion train. The milepost measures 95 miles from London St Pancras via Corby. *1 September 1999*

Left **Hellifield:** Thirteen bogies is a heavy load for this class of engine, and after an unscheduled stop to raise boiler pressure for the climb to Blea Moor summit, No 60800 departs with a Preston to Carlisle train. The heavy load was also taking its toll on the water supplies, and a further stop was made near Artengill where the tender was filled from a mountain stream!

Note the catchpoints in the foreground, which have claimed at least one victim. No 70003 was derailed here in the 1960s – see page 79 of *The Twilight of Steam* by Les Nixon (SLP 1 85794 168 3). *28 December 2001*

Below **Washwood Heath:** After a brief stop at Landor Street for a crew change, *Green Arrow* departs with a Banbury to York train. The signal box only controls the marshalling yard, not the main line. *16 June 2001*

Right **Barrow Hill:** Following a water stop, No 60800 gets under way again with a Derby to York special. The preserved former Staveley roundhouse is named after this small Derbyshire village. *25 August 2000*

Below **Seamer West:** The tracks are sprayed with weed-killer, but embankments are only cut if safety is compromised. It was just possible, however, to get a clear view above the lineside undergrowth of No 60800 on its way to Scarborough with a special day excursion train. *12 September 1999*

British Railways Standard locomotives

4MT Class 'Mogul'

Above **Trehafod:** Steam train and mining museum – No 76079 passes the Rhondda heritage park with a Cardiff to Treherbert special. *2 September 2001*

Above right **Sugar Loaf:** With thirteen on, it's unlikely that you will ever see a bigger passenger train than this on the Central Wales line. No 76079 pilots 'Black Five' No 45407 (as 45157) up the grade with a Newport (South Wales) to Wolverhampton special. *8 September 2001*

Right **Craven Arms:** The same locomotives and the same train are seen later that day at the former Bishops Castle junction site. Incorporated into the old British Railways standard express passenger headlamp code on this occasion, but more usually displayed separately in the centre, the high-intensity headlight now required to be carried on all trains has changed sides since the previous photograph. *8 September 2001*

4MT Class

Carnforth: Running as No 75019, No 75014 passes the Furness & Midland Junction signal cabin with a Preston to Grange-over-Sands train. Withdrawn from service at 11A Carnforth shed in August 1968, the real No 75019 was scrapped at Campbell's yard, Airdrie, in November 1968. *13 March 1998*

Above **Loch Eilt:** Well away from the Road to the Isles, which follows the opposite shore, this view is seen only by hill-walkers and railway enthusiasts. No 75014 passes with a Fort William to Mallaig train. *1 September 1995*

Below **Glenfinnan:** No 75014 departs with a Fort William to Mallaig special. The steam train stops for 20 minutes at the station so that passengers can make a brief visit to the West Highland railway museum. *30 August 1995*

Left **Shrewsbury:** The aesthetically pleasing combination of Nos 75014 and 70000 *Britannia* passes Sutton Bridge Junction, double-heading a Shrewsbury to Exeter St David's train. Note the lampman changing the oil lamps on the semaphore signals. *8 April 1995*

Below **Ais Gill:** Within a mile of the much celebrated summit, running in the traditional formation with the bigger, more powerful locomotive as the train engine, Nos 75014 and 70000 double-head a Carlisle to Liverpool Lime Street special. *31 March 1995*

Right **Chorleywood:** Hail to the steam train! The booking hall clerk abandons her post to greet the crew of No 75014, with an Amersham to Watford special on the southbound Metropolitan line. *19 May 1996*

Below **Chorleywood:** Out of use and somewhat neglected, the former Metropolitan signal box remains in situ as No 75014 passes with a Watford to Amersham train. *18 May 1996*

Findhorn Viaduct: At a location that makes a caption superfluous, No 75014 crosses the viaduct with an Inverness to Edinburgh train as the fireman puts a few shovelsful around the box for the climb to Slochd summit. *12 October 1997*

Right **Dalwhinnie:** The arrival of a steam train on the Highland main line does not appear to have created much excitement. After a brief stop No 75014 gets under way again with an Inverness to Edinburgh train, the same excursion as seen opposite earlier in the day, watched from the top of the embankment by two young ladies. *12 October 1997*

Below **Dalnaspidal:** No 75014 climbs to Druimachdair with an Edinburgh to Inverness train. Confident in the engine's capabilities the crew are sheltering inside their cab from the wind and rain. *4 October 1997*

Fort William: Ubiquitous British Railways Standard Class 4MT No 75014 is at Inverlochy, just north of the motive power depot, with a Fort William to Mallaig train. *25 August 1996*

Right **Fort William:** No 75014 shunts empty coaching stock at the carriage and wagon sidings. The gentleman on the footplate is David Richards, the well-known enthusiast and Preserved Steam on Video (PSOV) cameraman. *22 September 2000*

Below **Fort William:** No 75014 departs for the shed yard with empty coaching stock. The diesel-hauled overnight sleeper for London Euston is stabled in the siding on the right. *26 August 1996*

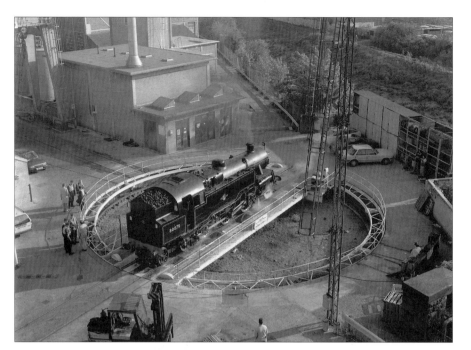

4MT Class Tank

Left **Bristol Bath Road:** After replenishing its coal and water supplies, No 80079 awaits the arrival of the coaching stock for a Bristol Temple Meads to Exeter St David's train. The turntable has since been sold to the Severn Valley Railway and moved to Bridgnorth. *1 May 1994*

Below **Skipton:** At the former engine shed site, No 80080 departs with a train arranged at short notice to position the engine and coaching stock at Carlisle for crew training. The semaphore signals have since been removed and the chimney in the background demolished in a much changed location following the installation of overhead line equipment for the electrification of services to Leeds and Bradford, among other places. *20 February 1993*

Right **Thorpe Culvert:** No 80080 passes with an afternoon Boston to Skegness train. In the 'off' position the somersault signal has the semblance of a lower-quadrant. *10 April 1993*

Below **Bellwater Junction:** Hurrying along the straight, No 80080 heads a Nottingham to Skegness train. The signalman has returned the somersault signal to the 'on' position before the last coach has passed. *3 May 1993*

Above **Whitchurch (Salop):** Designed for short-haul local services, and with good rear visibility for running bunker-first, the Standard tank engines are not well suited to long-distance railtours, due to the limited water-carrying capacity, although the small coal bunker is less of a problem as extra fuel can be accommodated in the support coach. No 80079 heads a Crewe to Stourbridge Junction train; this particular railtour was routed via Hereford, but the steam locomotive failed at Shrewsbury. *4 May 1998*

Below **Rugby:** Sadly the vast roof covering the platforms is being dismantled and this will be the last glimpse of steam before the remaining section is completely removed. No 80098 grinds to a halt, held by the signals, with a Northampton to Market Harborough train. *17 September 2000*

Right **Avonmouth:** No 80079 is on a Severn Beach to Bristol Temple Meads train, passing through a somewhat neglected area, although the station has been well maintained. *21 March 1999*

Below **Forders Sidings:** The brickworks established here by Forders have long since closed, but the sidings remain in use as a waste disposal terminal for the landfill site at the old clay pits. No 80079 passes with a Bedford to Bletchley train. *21 December 1996*

Above **Coalville:** Crossing over to the up line at the end of a single-track section, No 80079 and 80098 pass Mantle Lane signal box, double-heading a Birmingham to Crewe railtour. Passenger services here ceased in 1964, but the railway remains open for stone trains from the local quarries following the demise of the mining industry. *16 October 1999*

Below **Manton Junction:** Nos 80079 and 80098 are seen again double-heading a Leicester to London train on the up Kettering line. The Kettering and Manton line was formerly part of a through route from London St Pancras to Nottingham Midland via Corby; the section beyond Melton Mowbray is now the Old Dalby research track. *1 May 1999*

Right **Teignmouth:** The sea wall here is maintained by the railway and the huge boulders on the right have been added as an extra layer of protection so the residents of the cliff-top house need not worry too much about land erosion. No 80098 emerges from the short Parson's Tunnel with an early morning Exeter St David's to Newton Abbot train. *29 April 2000*

Below **Cockwood Harbour:** In late afternoon sunshine, No 80098 runs along the causeway with an Exeter St David's to Newton Abbot train. Some local people would rather own a boat than a car, and the moorings here are very much sought after. *29 April 2000*

5MT Class

Above **Aynho Junction:** As No 73096 passes with a Guildford to Stratford-upon-Avon train, the abandoned signal box awaits its fate. *13 September 1998*

Below **Salisbury:** At full blast, No 73096 crosses Clarendon Park Viaduct, near Petersfinger, with a Salisbury to Alton train. *15 March 1998*

Right **Canterbury West:** No 73096 departs for the sidings with empty coaching stock. Still operational, the massive signal box spanning the tracks survives. *17 July 1999*

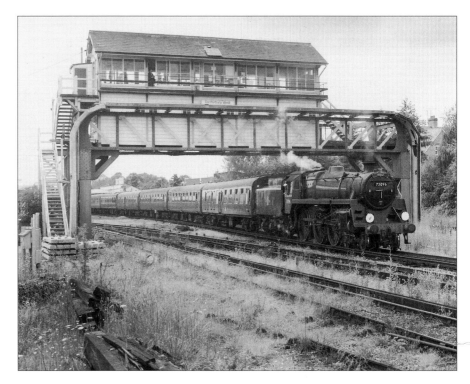

Below **Worcester Shrub Hill:** No 73096 departs with a train for Alton on the up main line. The signal cabin and semaphores from Great Western days remain in use. *24 April 1999*

7P Class

Bearley Junction: Listed in the 1951 Ian Allan *ABC* as the only 'Jubilee' with no name, No 45700 had relinquished its title to the leader of the new Standard Class 7P 'Pacifics' introduced that year. No 70000 *Britannia* is seen here with a Didcot to Stratford-upon-Avon special. The 'Jubilee' was later re-named *Amethyst* as a tribute to the RN ship involved in the famous Yangtze incident. *11 April 1993*

Above **Fenny Compton:** Leaning into the curve, No 70000 heads past with a Didcot to Derby train. The track layout has been revised, but semaphore signals remain and there is still much of interest for the railway enthusiast to see here. *12 March 1995*

Below **Ely:** *Britannia* is seen with a Cambridge to Kings Lynn special, rekindling memories of the day back in 1952 when, still almost new, the locomotive hauled the funeral train of King George VI up to London from Kings Lynn. *19 October 1991*

Rhyl: Not quite the way it was in the mid-1960s, by which time No 70000 was a 5A Crewe North engine, *Britannia* is still displaying the 30A Stratford shed code carried on most, if not all, of its main line excursions, in this case a Holyhead to Crewe train. *5 July 1992*

Right **Cogload Junction:** We are 138 miles from London Paddington via Newbury, as No 70000 passes with a Paddington to Taunton train. The route via Box (and Bristol) is more than 20 miles longer. *2 March 1996*

Below **Thetford:** *Britannia* is operating a Finsbury Park to Norwich Thorpe train. Little appears to have changed here since the 1950s when 15 of the then new Standard Class 7P 'Pacifics' were allocated to this Region. *23 March 1996*

8P Class

Tebay: Running at 60 miles per hour in accordance with the rules of engagement, the winner of the so-called Shap time trials, calculated on the engine's estimated drawbar horsepower, No 71000 *Duke of Gloucester*, begins the fear-inspiring climb with a Crewe to Carlisle special. As well as the gradient, the calculation takes into account the gross weight and speed of the train. *2 October 1995*

Howe & Co's Siding: No 71000 passes with a Carlisle to Blackburn train. The siding has been removed but there is still a goods loop and the former Midland Railway signal box remains. *6 August 1994*

Crowdundle: Running late due to delays caused by frozen points, on a day of temperatures well below zero Celsius, *Duke of Gloucester* passes with a Carlisle to Crewe train. *27 December 1995*

Directory of featured locomotives

Class	Locomotive		Built	Wheel arrangement	Pages
Great Western Railway locomotives					
'City'	3440	*City of Truro*	1903 Swindon	4-4-0	6-7
'Hall'	4936	*Kinlet Hall*	1929 Swindon	4-6-0	8, 10, 11
	4965	*Rood Ashton Hall*	1929 Swindon	4-6-0	9, 11
	5972	*Olton Hall*	1937 Swindon	4-6-0	11
'Castle'	5029	*Nunney Castle*	1934 Swindon	4-6-0	8, 10, 12-15
'King'	6024	*King Edward I*	1930 Swindon	4-6-0	16-21
'Modified Hall'	6998	*Burton Agnes Hall*	1949 Swindon	4-6-0	22-23
'Manor'	7802	*Bradley Manor*	1938 Swindon	4-6-0	24-25
	7819	*Hinton Manor*	1939 Swindon	4-6-0	24
Southern Railway locomotives					
'S15'	828		1927 Eastleigh	4-6-0	26-27
'West Country'	34016	*Bodmin*	1945 Brighton	4-6-2	31
	34027	*Taw Valley*	1946 Brighton	4-6-2	28-31
'Merchant Navy'	35005	*Canadian Pacific*	1941 Eastleigh	4-6-2	35, 37, 39
	35028	*Clan Line*	1948 Eastleigh	4-6-2	32-34, 36-39
London Midland & Scottish Railway locomotives					
2MT	46441		1950 Crewe	2-6-0	40-41
5MT 'Mogul'	2968		1934 Crewe	2-6-0	42-43
5MT 'Black Five'	44767		1947 Crewe	4-6-0	45, 46, 49, 51, 53
	44871		1945 Crewe	4-6-0	49
	45110		1935 Vulcan Foundry	4-6-0	47, 48, 50, 53
	45407		1937 Armstrong Whitworth	4-6-0	44, 46-48, 51, 52, 54-57, 72, 103
6P 'Jubilee'	45596	*Bahamas*	1935 North British	4-6-0	49, 58-61
8P 'Princess Royal'	6201	*Princess Elizabeth*	1933 Crewe	4-6-2	63, colour i, colour viii
	46203	*Princess Margaret Rose*	1935 Crewe	4-6-2	62-65
8P 'Coronation'	46229	*Duchess of Hamilton*	1938 Crewe	4-6-2	66, 67, 69
	6233	*Duchess of Sutherland*	1938 Crewe	4-6-2	2, 67-69, colour ii-iii
8F	48151		1942 Crewe	2-8-0	70, 71, 73-77
	48773		1940 North British	2-8-0	71-73, 76
London & North Eastern Railway locomotives					
'A2'	60532	*Blue Peter*	1948 Doncaster	4-6-2	78-79
'A3'	4472	*Flying Scotsman*	1923 Doncaster	4-6-2	80-87
'A4'	60007	*Sir Nigel Gresley*	1937 Doncaster	4-6-2	89-93
	60009	*Union of South Africa*	1937 Doncaster	4-6-2	1, 88, 92, 93, colour iv-v
'B1'	61264		1947 North British	4-6-0	94-95, colour vi-vii
'K1'	62005		1949 North British	2-6-0	94, 96, 97, colour vi-vii
'V2'	60800	*Green Arrow*	1936 Doncaster	2-6-2	98-101
British Railways Standard locomotives					
4MT	75014		1951 Swindon	4-6-0	104-111
4MT 'Mogul'	76079		1957 Horwich	2-6-0	52, 102-103
4MT Tank	80079		1954 Brighton	2-6-4T	112, 114-116
	80080		1954 Brighton	2-6-4T	112-113
	80098		1954 Brighton	2-6-4T	114, 116, 117
5MT	73096		1955 Derby	4-6-0	118-119
7P	70000	*Britannia*	1951 Crewe	4-6-2	106, 120-123
8P	71000	*Duke of Gloucester*	1954 Crewe	4-6-2	124-126

Index of locations

Acknowledgements

For their help in compiling this book, the author would like to thank Peter Townsend, Mick Sanders and Will Adams from Silver Link Publishing Ltd; Chris Banks and Ken Fairey, for access to their locomotive archive records; Jeff Cogan, 'the voice of the tours' for providing the lineside timings; and the locomotive owners, tour operators, and railwaymen of all grades, whose professionalism made it possible.